100

BESIDE
STILL
WATERS

BESIDE
STILL WATERS

GIEN KARSSEN

NAVPRESS

A MINISTRY OF THE NAVIGATORS
P.O. Box 6000, Colorado Springs, Colorado 80934

The Navigators is an international, evangelical Christian organization. Jesus Christ gave His followers the Great Commission to go and make disciples (Matthew 28:19). The aim of The Navigators is to help fulfill that commission by multiplying laborers for Christ in every nation.

NavPress is the publishing ministry of The Navigators. NavPress publications are tools to help Christians grow. Although publications alone cannot make disciples or change lives, they can help believers learn biblical discipleship, and apply what they learn to their lives and ministries.

Cover art: National Gallery of Art; "Winter Harmony" by John H. Twachtman

Illustrations: Mark Chickinelli

Unless otherwise identified, Scripture quotations are from the *Holy Bible: New International Version,* © 1978 by the International Bible Society, and used by permission of Zondervan Bible Publishers. Other versions quoted are *The Amplified Bible* (TAB), Old Testament, © 1962, 1964 by Zondervan Publishing House, and used by permission; the *King James Version* (KJV); *The Living Bible* (TLB), © 1971 by Tyndale House Publishers, Wheaton, Illinois, and used by permission; and the *New American Standard Bible* (NASB), © The Lockman Foundation 1960, 1962, 1963, 1968, 1971, 1972, 1973, 1975, and 1977.

Printed in the United States of America

(Originally published in the Netherlands as *Op Zoek Naar Rust,* © 1985 by Gien Karssen. Published by Buijten & Schipperheijn, Amsterdam. ISBN: 90-6064-563-4.)

CONTENTS

TO MY SISTERS

Wil Spijksma
Siny Davidson
Manny Veenhuizen

with whom I had the privilege to grow up in a
true Christian home where we first experienced
the peace that God gives.

AUTHOR

Gien Karssen, whose home is in The Netherlands, is the author of *Her Name Is Woman* (Books One and Two), *The Best of All,* and *Getting the Most Out of Being Single.* She is a Navigator representative living in The Hague, and has personally ministered to women throughout Europe for many years.

For Thou hast created us
for Thyself,
and our heart cannot be quieted
till it may find
repose in Thee.
SAINT AUGUSTINE

PREFACE

In many ways, rest and peace are rare commodities. We in the West should be grateful that since 1945, the end of World War II, the struggle for peace has showed some results. In many other places, peace is sorely missing. Though government leaders make all kinds of promises for peace, they are incapable of bringing it about. Summit conferences often increase world tensions instead of decreasing them. The dismal result is that since 1945 there have been many wars in which millions have lost their lives.

Within the borders of many countries there is a passionate thirst for rest. The results of peace efforts are sometimes favorable, but often times not. Sometimes much is achieved. At other times, the results are unemployment, riots, and strikes. These disturb the peace on the streets and the rest in the homes. In many countries there is great unrest as a result of catastrophies or threatening starvation.

The struggle for peace goes on in many families. There are those homes that, because of the efforts given to it, still function as havens of calm and rest. But in many others, the situation is less hopeful. Cares, tension, indifference, and helplessness drive husbands and wives, parents and children, apart. The way to peace seems to be blocked. Small wonder that many people don't see a way out of the problems.

Restlessness and discord, the distinctive marks of our time, have their roots in the distant past. They entered the world when the relationship between man and his Creator was broken. In the following fifty-two meditations (one for each week of the year) you will read about the source of discord and the rest that each of us sorely needs, both for inner healing and to be able to function effectively within our surroundings.

The Bible shows clearly that peace and rest are utterly dependent on relationships—with God, with people around us, and with ourself. The peace promised by the angels at Christ's birth depends on a relationship that we unfortunately have neglected too often (see my meditation on Luke 2:14).

Who is not searching for rest? Though we differ in personality, background, and circumstances, our need for peace is the same. Will you accompany me through the Bible on my search for peace? May you soon find yourself walking beside still waters.

1 A RESTING PLACE

*Then he [Noah] sent out a dove from him,
to see if the water was abated from the
face of the land; but the dove found no
resting place for the sole of her foot, so she
returned to him into the ark; for the water
was on the surface of all the earth. Then
he put out his hand and took her, and
brought her into the ark to himself.*

GENESIS 8:8-9, NASB

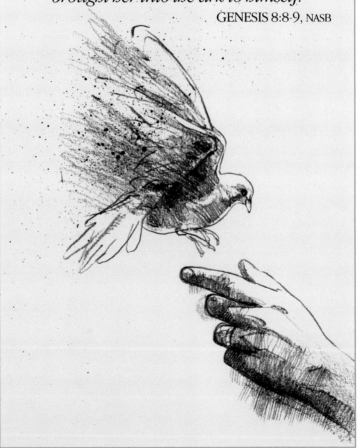

A single lonely bird hovered over a submerged world. Below her were the results of the catastrophic flood. There was nothing to be seen but water. The world below her was desolate and seemingly without a future. Nowhere could she find a place to hold on to, to set down her tiny foot. She found no rest.

Yet the dove that fluttered around purposelessly was less lonely than she appeared to be. Noah—his name means "he who will bring rest"—had not forgotten her. He waited for her return. When the bird came, she found an outstretched hand, ready to take her into the safety of the ark. Together they were on their way to a new future. The submerged earth would be habitable again.

We can be compared with this dove. We feel lonely and forsaken. We flutter around in a world that increasingly offers less to hold on to in every way. We see little hope for humanity. Spiritually and emotionally we find no rest.

Yet there is Someone who cares about us, who watches closely for each individual: GOD! Through Him we can find rest in spite of the catastrophes that harass the world. He offers us a place to stand, and hope, even in an apparently lost world. He offers a new beginning to those of us who return to Him.

=========== *PRAYER* ===========

Lord, I thank You that in this turbulent world You offer rest to every person who comes to You. My heart is full of unrest and fear. Therefore I come to You. Please give me Your rest. Amen.

2 WORK AND REST

*Work six days only, and rest the seventh;
this is to give your oxen and donkeys a
rest, as well as the people of your
household—your slaves and visitors.*

*For in six days the Lord made the heaven,
earth, and sea, and everything in them,
and rested the seventh day; so he blessed
the Sabbath day and set it aside for rest.*

EXODUS 23:12, 20:11, TLB

To work is a divine command. But to rest is no less a divine command. People and animals both need regular breaks from work and busyness to regain strength.

Rest refreshes both body and spirit.

Rest produces vitality.

Rest gives new strength physically, emotionally, and spiritually.

The Creator instituted the cycle of day and night. Additionally, He thought one day per week would be necessary as a pause after working for six. People belonging to one's household, even the animals, had to share in that rest.

The Lord Himself set the example. He rested on the seventh day after creating the world. That day—Saturday—had to be set apart by His people. It was to be a day of rest and a day to occupy themselves with the things of God.

After the resurrection of Jesus Christ, Christians chose the first day of the week—Sunday—to dedicate themselves to God and to gather new strength for the week and the work to come.

PRAYER

Lord, teach me the proper balance between work and rest. Help me to follow Your example and to allow myself the rest I need physically, emotionally, and spiritually. While I am doing this, guide my thoughts in order to know You better. Amen.

3 AT REST ABOUT THE FUTURE

And He [the Lord] said,
"My presence shall go with you,
and I will give you rest."
Then he [Moses] said to Him,
"If Thy presence does not go with us,
do not lead us up from here."

EXODUS 33:14-15, NASB

At eighty years of age, Moses faced one of the most difficult assignments of his life. He had to lead the Israelites, who had recently come out of captivity in Egypt, through the desert to the land of Canaan.

Moses was not without experience in leadership. He was also exercised in patience. He had grown up as a prince in the Egyptian court, then herded sheep for forty years in a desert. Yet, as he undertook this heavy task, he realized that his past experiences were insufficient. Also, in making and worshiping a golden calf, the people had just proved how unpredictable they were. How quickly they exchanged their God for an idol.

Moses was at rest only after receiving God's promise that He would go with Moses and the people.

The journey proved to be difficult. Moses met with disappointments and unexpected setbacks. Because of the unbelief of the people, it took much longer than necessary to reach their destination. Heat and drought, scarcity of food, and need for water tested the people severely.

Yet there was rest in Moses' heart, in spite of an existence full of unrest. His prayer was answered: God's presence moved ahead of him. So Moses completed his task, not in his own strength, but with God's help. Such reliance on God gives a man rest.

PRAYER

Lord, like Moses, I am not up to the task ahead of me. I feel burdened, uncertain, reluctant. Grant me the privilege of Your presence so that my heart will be at rest in spite of future responsibilities and tensions. Amen.

4 NATURE AT REST

When you [Israelites] come into the land I
am going to give you, you must let the land
rest before the Lord every seventh year. For
six years you may sow your field, . . . but
during the seventh year the land is to lie
fallow before the Lord, uncultivated . . .
for it is a year of rest for the land.

LEVITICUS 25:2-5, TLB

Thus the word of the Lord
spoken through Jeremiah came true,
that the land must rest for seventy years
to make up for the years
when the people refused
to observe the Sabbath.

2 CHRONICLES 36:21, TLB

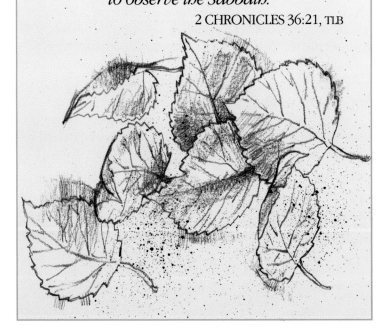

The land, like men and animals, needs to regain its strength. God therefore appointed regular times of rest for its soil. He appointed stewardship of the land to man, who also was to enjoy its fruit. God said to him "The seventh year . . . is a year of rest for the land."

God's people acted upon that command with indifference. They gave the land no pause to recover. The results of that disobedience were bitter, not only for the soil, but for the people as well. The Israelites were driven from their country. They were dispersed for many years until the land received its needed years of rest.

God watches over His Word and His creation. Even today, He keeps track of what people do with both.

=========== *PRAYER* ===========

Lord, I realize that You want to be obeyed in regard to nature around me. Give me a mind to seek and to do Your will within my responsibilities. Amen.

5 ACCEPTANCE OF GOD'S PEACE

The Lord bless you and keep you; the Lord make his face shine upon you and be gracious to you; the Lord turn his face toward you and give you peace.

NUMBERS 6:24-26

The above words may be familiar because this blessing is still pronounced in many churches today. But do you grasp its full magnitude? Do you realize who is speaking? It is the Lord, the Creator. His very name and character guarantee that He can give the promised peace. He graciously wants to bestow this on us.

But everything has its price. Peace is no exception. It cannot be bought with money, yet a high price was paid for it. It cost Someone His life! The Son of God died on a cross in order that there would be peace between God and men. He died to reconcile people one with another and with oneself.

So peace is a gift. It is given to those who want to accept it and who meet its conditions. Peace can never be separated from a personal relationship with God. It branches out to all aspects of our lives.

The offer of peace can be trusted. God is its guarantee. Whether we personally enjoy this peace is entirely in our own hands. God extend the offer. The acceptance depends on us.

PRAYER

Lord, I thank You that Your offer of peace is still valid today. Thank You for Jesus Christ, who paid the price with His life, that I can have peace with You. I accept Jesus' gift. Amen.

6 GRATITUDE FOR REST

*But you [Israel] will . . . settle in the land
the Lord your God is giving you as an
inheritance, and he will give you rest from
all your enemies around you. . . . Then to
the place the Lord your God will choose as
a dwelling for his Name—there you are to
bring everything I command you: your
burnt offerings and sacrifices, your tithes
and special gifts, and all the choice possessions you have vowed to the Lord. And
there rejoice before the Lord your God.*

DEUTERONOMY 12:10-12

*Praise be to the Lord, who has given rest to
his people Israel just as he promised. Not
one word has failed of all the good promises he gave through his servant Moses.*

1 KINGS 8:56

A life full of unrest lay behind the Israelites as they arrived in the Promised Land. For forty years they had wandered through the desert. They had fought enemies from within—disobedience and ungratefulness. And they had been involved in hostilities with the people through whose territories they passed.

In Canaan the former nomads became a settled nation. God had been true to every one of His promises. Not one word remained unfulfilled.

During the rest the Israelites enjoyed, they carefully considered God's service again. For years they had served Him in a movable sanctuary, a tent. Now He desired to live among them and be worshiped in one place.

In their need in the past the Israelites had called upon God and made solemn promises to Him. Now was the time to rejoice, but also to keep their vows. Joy about their redemption and reaching their destination must express itself in gratitude.

That gratitude was costly: it required the sacrifice of some precious livestock and the return of ten percent of each family's income. Gratitude that costs nothing is worth nothing.

God keeps His word. Therefore, He expects people to react in obedience and thankfulness. He loves men and women who do this. Obedience and gratitude enlarge our heart for God and give us rest.

PRAYER

Lord, You truly have been faithful to me in the past. I thank You. To show my gratitude, I want to worship You with an offering of my time and talents, and a portion of my income, for Your service. Help me to fulfill this vow. Amen.

7 BLESSING OR CURSE

Among those nations you [Israel] will find no repose, no resting place for the sole of your foot. There the Lord will give you an anxious mind, eyes weary with longing, and a despairing heart.

DEUTERONOMY 28:65

Those who pursue us are at our heels; we are weary and find no rest.

LAMENTATIONS 5:5

God's desire had been to set Israel "high above all the nations on earth" (Deuteronomy 28:1). He wanted to bless them abundantly in every way. He promised to open the heavens, the storehouse of His bounty, for them. There was only one condition: obedience. Just as obedience would be followed by blessings and rest, so disobedience would be followed by curses and unrest. God placed before His people a choice. Their decision determined the future.

From the time the Israelites went into exile in Babylon, until today, they have known little relief. They have found no rest physically, emotionally, or spiritually. They have become dispersed over the entire earth, reviled, driven into the gas chambers of Auschwitz as animals to the slaughter.

The same Jerusalem over which Jeremiah cried in Lamentations houses an exhibition of the Jewish Holocaust during the Second World War. Those who visit there will never forget what they see. A nation did not listen carefully to the voice of the Lord and experienced terrible results.

The warning for us is that God will judge other nations and individuals similarly, according to their obedience. God is righteous; therefore He kept His word in the past. In the future He will likewise be faithful to Himself.

PRAYER

Lord, I realize that the choice between curses and blessings in my life depends on me. You will be faithful to Your word. You know how easily my heart wanders away from You. Help me to obey! Amen.

8 EMOTIONAL REST

The Lord grant that you [Orpah and Ruth] may find a home and rest, each in the house of her husband!

Then Naomi her mother-in-law said to Ruth, My daughter, shall I not seek rest or a home for you, that you may prosper?

RUTH 1:9, 3:1, TAB

The relationship between a mother-in-law and daughter-in-law is often a cause for sour jokes. But the story of Naomi and her daughters-in-law shows mutual love and caring for one another.

Lack of food had driven Naomi from Bethlehem to Moab. She had gone with her husband and two sons, who all died there. When Naomi heard that Bethlehem had food again, she left Moab to return to her country. She told Orpah and Ruth, her daughters-in-law, to go back to their parental homes, as widows used to do that in those days. Naomi desired that they establish their own families and find rest emotionally after much grief in the past.

Orpah complied, but Ruth decided to go with Naomi instead. Ruth also decided to serve Naomi's God: "Your people will be my people and your God my God" (Ruth 1:16).

Naomi imparted such a love for the God of Israel to her Gentile daughter-in-law that He became her God as well. Ruth understood that true rest is not to be found in your own family but in God.

The Lord honored Ruth's dedication. She found a new homeland, another husband, and her own family. Naomi shared in Ruth's newfound happiness. But most important of all, Ruth's heart found rest—in God!

PRAYER

Lord, thank You for Your help in times of trouble, for relatives and friends who seek our best. Thank You for open doors after times of sorrow and death. May I grow in dedication to You as a result of such times. Amen.

9 A PEACEFUL CONSCIENCE

Then David accepted from her hand what she [Abigail] had brought him and said, "Go home in peace. I have heard your words and granted your request."

1 SAMUEL 25:35

There are days when evil powers suddenly strike, wanting to harm us permanently. David experienced such a day. He had recently offered help and protection to Nabal, a wealthy herdsman. Instead of being rewarded, David was rudely rejected. He decided to get revenge. Nabal and all his colaborers would be slaughtered.

David overlooked the importance and responsibilities of his coming position. He was the anointed future king of Israel. This premeditated reckless deed would give him a bad name with his future subjects. It would deprive him of peace of conscience and peace with God.

Nabal's wife, Abigail, understood the danger. Tactfully she gave David both things that her husband denied him: recognition that was due him and food.

"Please, listen to me," she said. "When in the past people tried to kill you, God kept you from taking revenge. Leave it, therefore, to Him to judge Nabal's rude behavior. When God makes you king, your conscience should not be burdened with murder."

Abigail's words restored David to sound thinking. They opened his eyes to the error of his ways. He praised the Lord for Abigail's intelligent judgment.

When the day of evil comes upon us, when we, confused by negative thinking, are in danger of making a wrong decision, may we also meet someone who warns us, who shows us the right way, who has our good conscience at heart. That is a gift of peace from God.

PRAYER

Lord, may I be a loving and discerning friend when the evil day strikes people around me. May I be Your instrument of peace, helping them to have a peaceful conscience. Amen.

10 MAN OF PEACE

But you [David] will have a son who will be a man of peace and rest, and I [the Lord] will give him rest from all his enemies on every side. His name will be Solomon, and I will grant Israel peace and quiet during his reign.

1 CHRONICLES 22:9

What benefit emanates from a man of peace. Solomon—his name means "shalom," or "peace"—was such a man. After King David's reign of forty years, which was characterized by wars, the nation and the people enjoyed forty years of rest. During Solomon's reign there was peace in the nation and with other nations. Every citizen enjoyed the fruit and the shade of his own garden.

At the start of his reign, Solomon was a humble man. When he succeeded his father to the throne, he acknowledged that he was young and without experience. He said to God, "I am as a little child who doesn't know his way around. And here I am among Your own chosen people, a nation so great that there are almost too many people to count! Give me an understanding mind, so that I can govern Your people well" (see 2 Chronicles 1:9-10).

Solomon's prayer for wisdom was answered. He also received more than he asked for. God promised him riches and honor, more than any king before him had ever had and none after him would have.

Peace, such as that of Solomon, is badly needed by leaders of nations. Churches, organizations, businesses, and homes cannot do without it either. They flourish when peace springs forth from those men and women who carry responsibility.

Solomon is history, but God is alive. He is still available to people who don't feel equal to their tasks, who feel their capacities are lacking. Even today He gives more than we ask for—if we humbly approach Him in prayer.

=== *PRAYER* ===

Lord, how I desire to be a person who provides rest in this agitated world. May peace and quiet increasingly be the outflow of my life. Thank You that You are still alive today and hear my prayer. Amen.

11 WISE USE OF REST

But as soon as they [the Israelites]
were at rest, they again did
what was evil in your sight.
Then you abandoned them
to the hand of their enemies
so that they ruled over them.
And when they cried out to you again,
you heard from heaven,
and in your compassion
you delivered them time after time.

NEHEMIAH 9:28

It often proves to be less difficult to win a war than to live with peace afterward. Every person who lived through World War II and nursed high expectations about the enjoyment of peace will agree.

When the unrest of war, tension, or sorrow is replaced by a time of rest, much has to be done to spend it beneficially. A time of rest can be detrimental for a country and its people by weakening spiritual and moral values. To handle rest badly can lead to crime and drug addiction.

Rest can have a paralyzing influence. Our muscles weaken through lack of exercise. Too much rest keeps our spirits less alert. Our minds need constant stimulation for their development.

A person needs three attitudes to use a time of rest profitably: gratitude for previous blessings, a desire to correct past mistakes and prevent them in the future, and willingness to occupy himself constructively. The best way to prevent evil is by doing good. Good intentions by themselves are not sufficient to guarantee beneficial rest.

When our rest changes to unrest, we must return to God and appeal to His forgiveness and compassion. This is corrective living. Preventive living is obeying God's Word—the Bible—in order that we take the right road from the very beginning.

PRAYER

Lord, keep me from using easy times in the wrong way. Help me attend to positive spiritual and moral values. Teach me how to apply Your Word in every area of my life and how to increase my strength physically, emotionally, and spiritually. Amen.

12 THE PURPOSE OF UNREST

Why is life given to a man
whose way is hidden,
whom God has hedged in? . . .
What I [Job] feared has come upon me;
what I dreaded has happened to me.
I have no peace, no quietness;
I have no rest, but only turmoil.

My gnawing pains never rest.

JOB 3:23-26, 30:17

No wonder Job lamented that he had no rest. His body from head to toe had been stricken with painful sores that did not give him one moment of rest or freedom from pain.

Neither did his emotions give him rest. Job had lost every one of his ten children. Nearly all of his servants had been killed. He had lost more than 10,000 animals. All those calamities struck Job on the same day.

His wife and his best friends had interpreted his reaction to those terrible blows in the wrong way. That added to his unrest.

But worst of all, Job's restless spirit plagued him with questions about God. How could He forsake an honest and God-fearing man in such a way? That was what troubled Job.

Later, after God's personal intervention, Job realized that pain and grief can produce blessing. His trial of faith had produced cleansing, refining, and a better perspective on God. When that purpose had been achieved, his blessings returned. Job regained his health, doubled the possessions he had before, and became a father of ten more children.

But most important of all, his relationship with God deepened. Job said, "I had heard about you before, but now I have seen you" (Job 42:5).

When people or things suddenly fall away from us, and we are about to lose our inner rest and peace, we can learn from Job. He discovered that God can allow a man to be tested—for his good. Job also learned that God never leaves a man alone.

PRAYER

Lord, there are times that I don't understand Your leading in my life. Job's story teaches me to keep trusting You. You have a plan—for my good. May Satan be defeated in my life as he was in Job's life. Amen.

13 THE SHEPHERD OF REST

The Lord is my shepherd,
I [David] shall lack nothing.
He makes me lie down in green pastures,
he leads me beside quiet waters,
he restores my soul.

PSALM 23:1-3

David, a shepherd in his youth, knew that if a sheep stayed close to his shepherd, nothing wrong would happen to him. In Psalm 23 David did not speak as a shepherd, but as one of the flock. His life, more than that of most people, had known peaks and valleys. But in spite of critical and emotion-filled circumstances, he had experienced rest. He knew through faith and experience that without the Good Shepherd, he would not have survived. He was convinced that the Lord, the Shepherd of Israel, was also his personal Shepherd. This gave him rest: "There is nothing further I desire," he said.

In John 10 Jesus called Himself the Good Shepherd who lays down His life for His sheep, who knows each sheep and calls it by name. The Good Shepherd bought His sheep with His life: He shed His blood for them.

In spite of this, His sheep are exposed to the same dangers as other sheep. Christians are acquainted with struggles and tensions. They are confronted with sorrow and illness. Unfaithfulness, frustration, problems in the home and at work are familiar to them.

Yet there is a difference. The Good Shepherd carefully watches over his own sheep. He oversees every situation in the lives of any and all of His sheep. When a person falls or is struck down, He gently picks him up. The Good Shepherd cares and encourages. He provides rest in green pastures, by quiet waters.

Do you know the Lord as your Shepherd?

PRAYER

Lord, I often feel like a wandering sheep amid the tensions, struggles, and dangers of daily living. Please be my Shepherd and lead me beside Your quiet waters. Amen.

14 STILLNESS AFTER THE STORM

*Then they cried out
to the Lord in their trouble,
and he brought them out of their distress.
He stilled the storm to a whisper;
the waves of the sea were hushed.
They were glad when it grew calm,
and he guided them
to their desired haven.*

PSALM 107:28-30

The storm that one moment caused people to panic was the next moment changed into a quiet breeze. In their utter distress, the people cried to God, and He heard them. Such miracles happen in answer to prayer.

The seamen were not the only ones who experienced help in need. We read in this psalm of others, like the people who wandered in the desert (see verses 4-9). Those who know the inhospitable Negev Desert with its drought, sudden sandstorms, and unexpected torrents, understand the ghastly situation that was looming here. The modern-day tourist is still grateful when, coming from Jerusalem, he arrives safely in the port town of Eilat.

Through their own doing, others found themselves in prison because they despised God's Word and the counsel of the Most High. Still others undermined their health through their way of life and became very ill (verses 10-22).

Fortunately, distress drove these people to God: "Then they cried out to the Lord in their trouble, and he delivered them." In every recorded situation, a miracle happened after prayer. Deliverance came right away (see verses 6,13,19, and 28). God delivered His people out of deep trouble and brought them to places of rest.

PRAYER

Lord, thank You for the reminder of a haven of rest in times of deep trouble and sickness, whether such times are a result of my own wrong behavior or not. Thank you that You also hear my prayers when I call on You. Amen.

15 THE REST OF THANKSGIVING

The Lord is gracious and righteous;
our God is full of compassion.
The Lord protects the simplehearted;
when I was in great need, he saved me.
Be at rest once more, O my soul,
for the Lord has been good to you.

PSALM 116:5-7

The unknown author of Psalm 116 had gone through very unrestful times. He had been close to death and as a result had become fearful about his life after death. He cried to God: "O Lord, save me!" The Lord answered him and provided relief, rest from the tensions and troubles of life.

Looking back, the man arrived at some important conclusions. His problems worked positively for him. He became aware that neither circumstances or chance or good luck accounted for his deliverance—only God.

He discovered the value and the necessity of prayer: "I will call on him as long as I live" (verse 2).

He also learned gratitude: "How can I repay the Lord for all his goodness to me? . . . I will sacrifice a thank offering to you and call on the name of the Lord" (verses 12 and 17).

This man made promises to God that he wanted to fulfill, not secretly, but "in the presence of all his people." His experiences were many and troublesome, but there came deliverance and a time of rest in which to understand and give thanks for God's goodness.

PRAYER

"Praise the Lord, O my soul; all my inmost being, praise his holy name. Praise the Lord, O my soul, and forget not all his benefits. He forgives all my sins and heals all my diseases; he . . . crowns me with love and compassion" (Psalm 103:1-4). Praise the Lord! Amen.

16 THE PEACE OF THANKSGIVING

I hate and abhor falsehood
but I love your law. . . .
Great peace have they who love your law,
and nothing can make them stumble.
I wait for your salvation, O Lord,
and I follow your commands.

PSALM 119:163-166

Is it possible to love the law? Isn't the law cool and businesslike? Doesn't it include commandments or requirements we find hard to carry out?

One who thinks like this fails to appreciate the context of this psalm. The author used a variety of words to describe the law of God. Besides law, he called it statutes, precepts, decrees, commands, words, and promises.

Each of these words highlighted different aspects of the Word of God, which was sweeter than honey to him (verse 103), and provided the song of his life (verse 54). From early in the morning, through the day, even when he awoke at night, he meditated upon God's promises (verses 147-148). At midnight he gave thanks for them (verse 62).

This man was at peace in spite of constant dangers (verse 109) and many enemies (verse 157). This great inner peace did not depend on favorable circumstances, but on the certainty that he belonged to the Lord.

Adjusting our life to God's Word gives peace. It produces insight and balance between humility (verse 130) and proper self-esteem (verses 98-100). It gives courage to speak about our faith (verse 46). A person who lives in such a way walks in freedom (verse 45). The path of his life is peaceful and straight. He sees oncoming dangers and can guard against them in time.

Peace and rest in a world full of unrest. Standing erect when many stumble and fall: that can be the experience of those who love the Word of God and live accordingly. The enormous peace that is offered is the complete fulfillment of everything good and desirable. It is available to the lovers of God's Word!

PRAYER

Lord, honest heart-searching reveals how much I lack in this respect. Fill me with a great love for Your Word, in order that my life may produce the fruits thereof. Amen.

17 DELIBERATE SURRENDER

But I [David] have
stilled and quieted my soul;
like a weaned child with its mother,
like a weaned child
is my soul within me. . . .
Put your hope in the Lord
both now and forevermore.

PSALM 131:2-3

David knew the tensions and insecurities of life through and through. He experienced disappointments with others and with himself. As the youngest of the family, he felt pressure from his older brothers. He was repeatedly threatened with death, both as a shepherd and while making music at the royal court of King Saul.

During a period of wandering with a group of men who expected leadership from him, he often didn't know where their next meal was to come from. Problems with his wife and children did not pass his doorstep. David's greatest sorrow, no doubt, was over his own unfaithfulness with Bathsheba.

It is not known when David wrote the above lines. He probably had this experience more than once during his life. This fervidly active man, who knew the turbulence of life from personal experience, also knew about the rest that faith offers: "My soul finds rest in God alone" (Psalm 62:1). "Find rest, O my soul, in God alone" (Psalm 62:5).

Rest here refers to the leveling of ploughed ground. It is the rest of the soil after it is thoroughly furrowed. It is the rest, the quiet, after the storm. One can scarcely think of a greater difference than the unrest of stormy life and the rest of a weaned child with its mother. The child is satisfied because its mother is close by. What a touching picture of confidence and total surrender.

"But I have stilled and quieted my soul." Surrender to God was for David a deliberate act of his will. He refused to give in to worry. He trusted God instead.

Like David, leave yourself, your work, and your family—responsibilities great and small—with God. Depend on His help.

David's life lies before us like an open book. We read about wedded bliss and marriage problems, about children being born and dying, about poverty and riches, about abuse and adoration, about humble work and extraordinary responsibilities. We look into the heart of a man who loved God passionately, but who, in spite of this, sinned grossly and tried to live without God's forgiveness.

David's extensive biography was recorded for us as a warning, and to give us courage. Like David, we should train ourselves to become still and quiet before God, under all kinds of circumstances. This practice is sorely needed by people with busy lives, who by nature are restless and nervous, who are easily and unduly caught up in the hurried times in which we live.

PRAYER

Lord, because I am leading a busy life, I often feel restless and nervous. Help me in the circumstances in which I find myself to deliberately bring my entire being to quietness and stillness with You. Amen.

18 THE PEACE OF OBEDIENCE

My son, do not forget my teaching,
But let your heart keep my commandments;
For length of days and years of life,
And peace they will add to you.

PROVERBS 3:1-2, NASB

What father doesn't desire a long and happy life for his son? What parent doesn't want a peaceful life for his child? (The word *son* was also used by a teacher to address his pupil.)

The choice is up to the child himself. A long and peaceful life comes from living by God's laws.

Godly living also results in optimal relationships with God and men. Deep inner peace abides in those people who involve God in all they do, who acknowledge Him in everything. And this peace grows. It becomes richer and deeper.

Proverbs reveals the great need in those times for practical daily wisdom, and for the realization that wisdom is found only with God. He alone is wisdom.

Nearly three thousand years have gone by since these words were written, a period in which the world situation has changed drastically. But people who consistently walk with God, and who are able to help others do the same, are still urgently needed.

Living according to the Bible results in blessing. Everything we need to know for our temporary well-being as well as for life hereafter is recorded in this Book. Reading, studying, meditating on, and applying it give peace. Its influence permeates every aspect of human life (read Proverbs carefully). The outlook of the world would be much brighter if parents would point to God's Word with great emphasis and conviction.

PRAYER

Lord, I easily forget Your teaching, and my heart tends to wander away from Your Word. Help me start again to study and apply it more consistently. Amen.

19 THE PEACE OF DISCIPLINE

The rod of correction imparts wisdom,
but a child left to itself
disgraces his mother. . . .
Discipline your son,
and he will give you peace;
he will bring delight to your soul.

PROVERBS 29:15,17

Solomon knew that discipline or correction would drive folly far from a child and impart wisdom. He said that a child should not be left to itself since it would disgrace its mother (verse 15).

A child raised in this way brings joy to its parents! The Bible confirms this by the example of the priest Eli. This man didn't rebuke his wicked sons. The results were corruption of worship, military defeat, and the downfall of Eli's entire family.

Psychologists say that children of parents who are insecure and inconsistent in their standards become frightened and restless. The permissiveness of many present-day parents does not prove their love, but rather hatred, according to the Bible.

Discipline or correction does not mean to lose self-control and beat a child or to lash him or her with words. To the contrary, the Scriptures exhort fathers not to make their children angry and resentful.

Solomon emphasized correction in the early years, to prepare children for their future place in society.

Your task as a parent is extremely heavy. And unfortunately you have but few positive examples to follow. You can learn, however, from the Father who had a Son—Jesus. He will give you strength and wisdom and rest.

PRAYER

Lord, the future of our world lies in the hands of those who are yet children. Instill in every parent's heart a desire to seek You for proper answers. May our youth consequently find security and rest in You. Amen.

20 MEANINGFUL EXISTENCE

So what does a man get
for all his hard work?
Days full of sorrow and grief,
and restless, bitter nights.
It is all utterly ridiculous.

ECCLESIASTES 2:22-23, TLB

Man has the need to work. And he is commanded to do so. He finds satisfaction therein, but it is the source of his concern and grief at the same time. Day after day he works hard to secure his existence. But even sleep brings him little rest, for his troubles keep following after him. A person who is honest with himself will admit that even the most interesting job doesn't give complete satisfaction, nor does a high bank account balance.

Why does man work hard? To earn the money he needs to buy food and clothing. Both are needed if man is to work, so he works harder to earn more money. Thus man lives in a vicious circle. No wonder the author of the above words exclaimed, "It is all utterly ridiculous!"

The wise preacher finally arrived at the conclusion that the only meaningful activity that truly satisfies is to fear God, to have a worshipful respect for Him. The heart of man is created so that it can find rest only in God.

Believing in such a way is no flight from reality. On the contrary, the greatest reality of all is that only a person who gets his sights properly set on God acquires the right perspective of his own existence. He experiences rest in spite of the many daily troubles and cares. Heavenly rest! That is why he can go on.

=========== *PRAYER* ===========

Lord, my life goal is to accomplish more than keeping up with the requirements of daily living. I want my life to count for You. Amid troubles and cares with which I am well acquainted, I want to experience a meaningful existence that honors You. Amen.

21 ONE HAND FULL OF REST

One hand full of rest is better than two
fists full of labor and striving after wind.

ECCLESIASTES 4:6, NASB

Better is a little with the fear of the Lord,
Than great treasure and turmoil with it.

PROVERBS 15:16, NASB

Chasing after wind, trying to catch it. No person in his right mind would ever do that. Such efforts would produce nothing. A little rest is preferable indeed compared to such foolishness.

The Bible is clear that true rest cannot be experienced apart from God. Solomon, the wisest man who ever lived, and author of the above statements, challenges us to take inventory. What are we striving after? What treasures do we try to accumulate? What will be the sum total of how we spend our days?

Questions that thrust themselves upon us are, Do I experience rest in what I am doing? Is what I occupy myself with of lasting value?

To work for our necessities is a must. To enjoy things that make life more pleasant is a gift from God. But is that the goal of our lives? If God has no place in our daily efforts, then our lives can be compared with striving after wind.

The Lord Jesus once told the story of a man who based his entire existence on the pursuit of pleasure. He was a man who did not consider God. His life ended poorly. On the day he stated his intention to enjoy his possessions, God said, "You fool! This very night you will die. Then you will get what you have prepared for yourself" (see Luke 12:16-21).

Jesus Christ told this parable to warn us. Remember, people who are warned ahead of time can offer no valid excuse.

PRAYER

Lord, keep me from being a fool who stakes his life primarily on temporary things. Search my heart, and reveal what my deepest motives are. What am I striving after? Then help me to focus my thoughts and deeds on things of everlasting value. Amen.

22 PRINCE OF PEACE

For to us a child is born,
to us a son is given,
and the government
will be on his shoulders.
And he will be called . . . Prince of Peace.
Of the increase
of his government and peace
there will be no end.

ISAIAH 9:6-7

The time is coming when newspapers, radio, and television will not be taken up with oppression in Eastern Europe and Southeast Asia anymore. Latin America and South Africa will no longer be hotbeds that threaten to set the world aflame. The Middle East will no longer threaten to explode at any moment. The Western world, Europe in particular, will not fear Russia any longer. The terror of atomic weapons will be expelled. The media will bring good news exclusively. A child will not wonder whether he or she will live to see adulthood.

That is the time of which Isaiah prophesied. The Prince of Peace will bring about eternal peace on earth, not only peace that ends wars between nations and disagreements among people, but peace in its true meaning, a shalom so rich that it is hard to capture in words.

This Prince of Peace has come in the person of a child. He is Jesus Christ, born in Bethlehem some seven centuries after Isaiah's prophecy. Jesus' birth provided a universal turning point in human history. Every date we read on our calendars or write on our correspondence refers to this event.

He is the One who brought Heaven and earth, God and man, together. He, the Prince of Peace, willingly gave His life to bring reconciliation and peace to people alienated from God. Such a peace will influence every aspect of their lives.

Peace in the world has to be preceded by peace in human hearts. Does the Prince of Peace rule in your heart and mind now? Is He your peace?

PRAYER

Lord, thank You that world peace, accompanied by justice and righteousness, is coming. Thank You for the glorious prospect that Satan will surrender to Jesus Christ. Thank You that Christ is my Prince of Peace. Amen.

23 LASTING REST

And it will be in the day when the Lord
gives you [Israel] rest from your pain and
turmoil and harsh service in which
you have been enslaved. . . .
The whole earth is at rest and is quiet;
They break forth into shouts of joy.

ISAIAH 14:3,7, NASB

Since Isaiah's prophecy, Israel has experienced only brief intervals of rest and peace. Time and again there have been wars and unrest. At times the nation has been close to annihilation. The Israelites lived in captivity in Babylon, and then were dispersed over the entire globe.

But these promises will be fulfilled. God speaks His words to do them. Presently the Jews live in their own country, but peace and rest are far away, for this nation and for all nations. The earth will not find rest until it is purified and renewed, governed by the Prince of Peace, Jesus Christ.

How unimaginably happy life will be in His Kingdom of Peace. Isaiah prophesied about this time when he said that swords will be beaten into plowshares and spears into pruning hooks (Isaiah 2:4). The time is coming when one nation no longer will fight another nation, when military academies and armed forces will be abolished.

Such an ideal situation will not come about through man, but by the Spirit of God. That Spirit is working right now to complete this grand plan, even though it hardly looks like that.

=========== *PRAYER* ===========

Lord, thank You for the promise that the time will come when all the earth is filled, as the waters fill the sea, with an awareness of the glory of the Lord. May that day soon be here! Amen.

24 STEP OF REST

This is what the Sovereign Lord,
the Holy One of Israel, says:
"In repentance and rest
is your salvation,
in quietness and trust
is your strength."

ISAIAH 30:15

Salvation and rest are concepts that belong together. Salvation—spiritual rescue from the consequences of sin—begins with conversion, a point at which a person turns back in repentance from the way he or she was going and moves in the opposite direction, the way that leads to God.

Such a turning around requires a definite choice. It is a deed of the will and the mind. Conversion is the first step in the right direction. The Lord God waits for people who repent and turn to Him, who surrender their lives and their futures to Him with complete trust.

The verse from Isaiah quoted above refers to Israel's rest as a nation. The rest we need most of all, however, is that of the heart. The New Testament shows the way. It clarifies that salvation, which is personal faith in Jesus Christ, is the only way to God. Jesus said of Himself, "I am the way and the truth and the life. No one comes to the Father except through me" (John 14:6).

True salvation means resting in God instead of in our own achievements. For people who do this, God becomes a Father. He makes His children strong with His power. Faith is the only power through which we can hold on in this life. This power supplies us with rest and confidence for the future.

This rest, with its accompanying blessings, is offered to us freely. It is up to us whether we accept or neglect the offer. The people to whom Isaiah spoke reacted negatively. Their rejection became their downfall. Let us not follow their example. That leads to nothing but unrest and ruin.

PRAYER

Lord, thank You for Jesus Christ and the salvation offered through His death and resurrection. Thank You for the rest of heart and mind He gives to people who accept Him as their Savior and Lord. May I not reject Him. Amen.

25 RESTLESS MAN WITHOUT GOD

But the wicked are like the tossing sea,
which cannot rest,
whose waves cast up mire and mud.
"There is no peace,"
says my God, "for the wicked."

ISAIAH 57:20-21

And to whom did God swear
that they would never enter his rest
if not to those who disobeyed?

HEBREWS 3:18

The Bible compares the life of the wicked with the restlessness of the sea—one wave chasing another, never finding a moment of rest. The wicked are those who disobey God, the ungodly. Their existence is not only without rest, it is also useless. Mire and mud are the result of their lives. There is no stability, color, or fragrance. The wicked are empty of content and beauty!

Scripture leaves no doubt about the fate of the wicked: "Woe to the wicked! Disaster is upon them! They will be paid back for what their hands have done!" (Isaiah 3:11). "The lamp of the wicked is snuffed out; the flame of his fire stops burning" (Job 18:5). "All his days the wicked man suffers torment" (Job 15:20). "But the way of the wicked is like deep darkness; they do not know what makes them stumble" (Proverbs 4:19).

How different is the life of a righteous, or godly, person. His life radiates wisdom and rest: "The path of the righteous is like the first gleam of dawn, shining ever brighter till the full light of day" (Proverbs 4:18).

What makes the difference between the wicked and the righteous? The godly person experiences rest because he has admitted that he cannot save himself. He has surrendered in obedience to God. God's rest fills his heart and life.

No man is born with righteousness. It is imparted to him by faith in the Righteous One, Jesus Christ. No man needs to live and die as a wicked, ungodly person. The offer of rest is available to everyone.

PRAYER

Lord, how meaningless and terrible is the lot of the ungodly. Open the eyes of many to their need of You. Though having found rest in You, I sometimes feel restless and unwilling to follow. Increase my desire to obey. Amen.

26 SOCIETY AT REST

This is what the Lord says:
"Stand at the crossroads and look;
ask for the ancient paths,
ask where the good way is,
and walk in it,
and you will find rest for your souls."

JEREMIAH 6:16

The prophet Jeremiah, in obedience to the Lord, had confronted the nation of Israel with its disobedience. Through Jeremiah, God pointed the way to peace, prosperity, and safety within a religiously and morally well-ordered life of the people—a society at rest. Such a society must continually ask the question, Are we on the good way? Have we followed the ancient paths, the ways in which God has led His people in the past and shown His faithfulness?

To guide His people, God the Creator had given them His law to live by: "It is to be with him [the king], and he is to read it all the days of his life so that he may learn to revere the Lord his God and follow carefully all the words of this law and these decrees" (Deuteronomy 17:19).

God's Word, written on parchment in those days, was in the possession of a privileged few. Those people had to know that Word in order to live accordingly and to teach it to others.

Today everyone can buy himself a Bible. Through its pages, God reveals His plans for men, His purposes for them after this life. That Book informs us of how we can walk with God, and get along with our fellowmen and ourselves. In brief, it is a guide we cannot do without to function properly and harmoniously and to live a happy life. Living according to this Book produces rest, even in a turbulent world full of unrest.

PRAYER

Lord, thank You for the availability of Your Word. Thank You that Your plans for my life now and for eternity are outlined therein. Bless the translation and distribution of the Bible worldwide in order that many will find rest for their souls. Amen.

27 PEACEMAKERS

*Also, seek the peace and prosperity of the
city to which I have carried you into exile.
Pray to the Lord for it, because if it
prospers, you too will prosper.*

JEREMIAH 29:7

Jeremiah wrote to the Israelites, who had been driven from their homeland into Babylon, and were living in exile in a far-away and heathen country. They had not heeded God's warnings or repented of their evil ways, even though Jeremiah had prophesied that they would live in exile seventy years. Young people would spend their entire lives in bondage. The older generation would never see their beloved country again.

Despondency, apathy, and fighting against the oppressive regime are the reactions one can expect under such circumstances. Such reactions, Jeremiah said, should not be allowed. On the contrary, the prophet urged the Israelites to behave positively. He told them to seek peace, that is, the well-being of their temporary home. He encouraged them to colabor for Babylon's prosperity, to conduct themselves as good citizens, to build homes, plant gardens, grow fruit trees, marry, and raise children.

Everyday living had to go on, but God did not leave the Israelites alone in their troublesome times (for which they were to blame). In spite of everything, life did not lose its meaning. God used negative circumstances for good.

Joseph is an example of this. Because of jealousy, he was sold by his brothers and taken to heathen Egypt. He found himself in the house of Potiphar, one of the king's high officials. The son of a free and wealthy sheep owner became a slave. When the wife of his master approached Joseph with immoral suggestions, he rejected her out of respect for God, his master, and himself. That led to prison, where he spent several years.

How did Joseph react? Did he complain? Did he allow self-pity? To the contrary. His faith in God stood the test. His attitude both in Potiphar's house and in prison resulted in blessing. He gained such respect as a prisoner that gradually the responsibility of all that was going on there was entrusted to him.

Through Joseph, God revealed to the king of Egypt that a great famine was coming. Joseph took practical measures to prepare for the famine and save the people among whom he lived against his free will. He also saved his own family. "And all the countries came to Egypt to buy grain from Joseph, because the famine was severe in all the world" (Genesis 41:57).

The peace of the Egyptians to whose well-being Joseph dedicated himself proved to be peace for the entire world. Suffering can be meaningful. God transformed Joseph's trials into something very good.

Relatively few people experience exile and imprisonment. But there are other circumstances that can make the future dark for each one of us.

Joseph's story proves that even in dark times God remains in command. Things are never beyond His control. People who trust Him, who under all circumstances continue to serve God, can stand hard times. They may even see them turn into blessings. They learn that such times offer opportunities not found in any other way. Peace is experienced fully when we work for the peace of others.

PRAYER

Lord, I want to seek and pray for the peace of the place where I live and work. I desire to be a positive influence by never losing sight of You, and by working for the peace of others, even in adverse circumstances. Amen.

28 HOPE FOR PEACE

*For I know the thoughts and plans
that I have for you, says the Lord,
thoughts and plans for welfare and peace,
and not for evil,
to give you hope
in your final outcome.*

JEREMIAH 29:11, TAB

The disaster, the deportation to Babylon, didn't befall the Israelites unexpectedly. Moses had predicted that resistance to God's commandments would result in dispersion among the nations. The people had ignored these warnings about sin and idolatry. So they experienced God's chastisement. He cannot be mocked.

Although circumstances ultimately turned out for good, the consequences of sin and apostasy remained intact. Jerusalem, the Holy City, was in the hands of a heathen oppressor. The Judean countryside was ravaged. Families were broken. Temple service was disturbed.

But in spite of their apostasy, God still cherished thoughts of welfare and peace for His people: "You will seek me and find me when you seek me with all your heart. I will be found by you, and will bring you back from captivity" (Jeremiah 29:13-14). God was willing to forgive sin, to show grace, to restore and reestablish the people.

We read in Romans 15:4 that "everything that was written in the past was written to teach us." This story teaches us that an individual or a nation cannot sin cheaply. May God keep us from missing precious opportunities because of disobedience, neglect, or unbelief. May we seek and enjoy the peace of obedience.

PRAYER

Lord, help me to carefully heed Your warnings, in order that I will not lose precious opportunities that will never come again. Amen.

29 PEACE WITHOUT ANSWERS

"Do not be afraid [Daniel], O man highly esteemed," he said. "Peace! Be strong now; be strong." When he spoke to me, I was strengthened and said, "Speak, my lord, since you have given me strength."

Daniel 10:19

As a boy living in exile in Babylon, Daniel had made a courageous decision to remain faithful to God in Gentile surroundings. Since his youth, God had given him great knowledge, understanding, and insight through visions and dreams. This earned Daniel great respect from five successive rulers. Through him God revealed His will to these rulers. Daniel's prayer life was remarkable. In spite of his busy days, he kept set times for prayer: "Three times a day he got down on his knees and prayed, giving thanks to his God" (Daniel 6:10). He maintained this habit even when it placed his life in great danger.

Daniel experienced many striking answers to prayer. He saw his friends step unscathed out of the flames of a fiery oven. When thrown in a den of lions himself, he saw these savage animals shut their mouths, doing him no harm.

Toward the end of his life, when he had acquired a high position and great influence, his increasing faithfulness and steadfastness of character were still unimpaired. But he was in great distress concerning the future of his people, which had been revealed to him in a vision. He wrestled with his God for three weeks and ate no food, but Heaven seemed to be deaf to his petition. When Daniel had prayed before about the sad state of his people, he had been answered immediately.

Then a heavenly messenger appeared, saying, "Since the first day that you set your mind to gain understanding and to humble yourself before your God, your words were heard, and I have come in response to them. But the prince of the Persian kingdom [Satan] resisted me twenty-one days" (Daniel 10:12-13). Satan, an opposer of God and thus an opposer of prayer, had held up the answer.

Daniel, feeling weak and helpless, had nearly collapsed when he saw the messenger. But the man's words gave Daniel new strength and peace.

The New Testament speaks clearly about the fight behind the scenes, the struggle in the heavenly realms (see Ephesians 6:10-18). Supernatural powers of evil are more active in our time than ever. Now, as in the past, they can be conquered only by prayer. Therefore, we should pray on every occasion, always in line with the wishes of the Holy Spirit.

If answers to our prayers are not forthcoming, then Daniel's experience can encourage us because it revealed what happens between God and Satan when people pray. This should give us perseverance at times when everything seems to be against us. It should encourage us not to give up.

PRAYER

Lord, I thank You for this insight into the struggle behind the scenes. May I learn from Daniel's experience to hold on in prayer, even when the answer is not forthcoming immediately. Amen.

30 A ROYAL INVITATION

"Come to me, all you who are weary and burdened, and I will give you rest."

MATTHEW 11:28

A more royal invitation was never given than Jesus' offer of rest for the soul, that part of us that was created for God and will live forever. This is the rest we cannot do without in order to function properly during our earthly stay and to gain access to eternal life to follow.

The invitation is extended to all, but especially to those who are weighed down under the burden of questions concerning God. There are no exceptions to this promise based on race, color of the skin, position in life, or age. Every individual can receive rest spiritually if he responds to the Person who extends the invitation: Jesus Christ. He must also surrender himself and believe in the forgiveness of his guilt.

The person who accepts Jesus' invitation in such a way becomes born again into a living relationship. He has found rest in his conscience, rest from the terrible power of sin, and rest in God.

The Danish sculptor Bertel Thorvaldsen shaped the inviting Christ in marble. Underneath he carved the words *Come to Me.* People who visit his museum in Copenhagen, Denmark, are reminded that after nearly two thousand years Jesus' offer of rest is still open and as welcome as when it was first given. Jesus says, "COME . . . and I will give you REST."

PRAYER

Lord, the burden and weariness of our times are more than many, including myself, can cope with. May Your invitation to come and find rest be accepted by us. Reach our minds, hearts and wills in a new way, in order that troubled individuals everywhere find rest in You. Amen.

31 A LIGHT BURDEN

"Take my yoke upon you and learn from me, for I am gentle and humble in heart, and you will find rest for your souls. For my yoke is easy and my burden is light."

MATTHEW 11:29-30

Christians have burdens to carry. Jesus is very clear about this. We, like everyone else, live in a world full of uncertainties, dangers, and losses. Adversity, unemployment, poverty, disease, and death do not bypass us.

The difference is that we do not need to carry our burdens alone. Christ offers to carry them with us. He determines how heavy our burdens should be. He sees to it that nothing will surpass our strength.

Jesus also offers rest to the entire person: spirit, soul, and body. It is the rest we need to carry out our life's work. Jesus' yoke is good for us. It is not a burden He imposes upon us. In fact, just the opposite is true. His yoke serves to ease the burden a Christian has to carry. Think of the yoke that is fitted across the necks of a pair of animals. Two oxen that are yoked together to pull a burden walk closely together; they fall in step with each other.

In the same way a Christian yoked to Christ walks through his day with God, doing his work very closely with Him. Whatever his experience, whether the road goes over mountain tops or through valleys, he experiences rest in spite of troubles and difficulties.

PRAYER

Lord, Your Word is clear that Christians are not exempt from hardship. Help me in the adversities of daily living to walk so closely to You that You carry my burden with me. Amen.

32 PHYSICAL REST

The apostles gathered around Jesus and reported to him all they had done and taught. Then, because so many people were coming and going that they did not even have a chance to eat, he said to them, "Come with me by yourselves to a quiet place and get some rest."

MARK 6:30-31

The disciples had exciting times behind them. They had been sent by Jesus to preach and to perform miracles. Now they had returned to tell the Master how His power had worked in them, how their message was accepted, how the sick were healed and devils cast out. They also needed encouragement, refreshment, and possibly correction.

Jesus noticed how exhausted the men were. Their work apparently had taken much spiritual and physical energy. The people gave them so little rest that the disciples scarcely found time to eat or be refreshed by a drink.

Jesus had experienced physical fatigue personally. He knew that his disciples now needed relaxation and refreshment. That is why He extended His invitation, "Come with me to a quiet place and get some rest."

The period of rest did not last long. It was limited to a few hours on a lake. But the disciples were freed briefly from their daily cares. They would never forget that Jesus was concerned about their physical welfare, and that He did something about it.

This is still true today. Jesus Christ became fully human to be able to understand man in every life situation, including when he is exhausted. Jesus is the giver of physical rest.

PRAYER

Lord, You know how exhausted I sometimes become from serving people, how all spiritual, mental, and physical strength can leave me. Thank You for the reminder to take time to relax. Amen.

33 AND ON EARTH, PEACE

*Suddenly a great company
of the heavenly host
appeared with the angel,
praising God and saying,
"Glory to God in the highest,
and on earth peace
to men on whom his favor rests."*

LUKE 2:13-14

Peace has never met with more interest than right now. Large crowds gather together to demonstrate for peace in many cities of the world. Banners, slogans, and chants ventilate the anxiety about the increasing war threat. Politicians, economists, and all kinds of scientists look for ways to prevent total annihilation of mankind. A continuous stream of books leaves the presses, and statements are issued regularly—all offering solutions.

Every year in Oslo, Norway, the Nobel prize for peace is awarded to people who so far have been unable to bring it about. Lebanon, which once housed the largest "peace army," bleeds from thousands of wounds received in actions of war.

While people everywhere dedicate themselves to the pursuit of peace, parents worry about their frightened little children who go to sleep afraid that the bomb may fall. Youth express their lack of hope for the future through apathy and vandalism. Adults are not any less afraid, dreading the catastrophe that may befall the earth. To get a grip on peace seems harder now than ever before.

Why this helplessness? For what reason, in spite of all these efforts, do threats of war increase?

Could it be because the origin and nature of peace are misunderstood? Has the pursuit of peace become the goal rather than peace itself? Have we forgotten that peace can only be enjoyed on condition? Do we realize that peace is more dependent on the attitude of the heart than on politics?

The Bible speaks more about peace than any other book does. It also points the way to real and lasting peace.

"Glory to God!" Thus started the angels' song, followed by "and on earth, peace." Peace stays away when we change the order. In the deepest sense, peace doesn't start with disarmament or reduction of atomic weapons. Peace starts by desiring to bring highest honor to God. World peace begins in the heart.

Peace is too many-sided and too fragile to be a product of human efforts alone. It is not achieved when the interest for peace itself is greater than for the Prince of Peace, who commands peace. It comes nearer after surrender to the Maker of Peace.

Peace is offered in a Person, in Jesus Christ, whose coming into the world the angels proclaimed. Any other peace—with oneself, with others, or with the world— results from that. There is no other hope of peace for East and West, for North and South.

Being concerned about the absence of peace is right. Searching for peace is commendable. But peace comes within our reach only when we seek it where it can be found: with God. When we give Him His rightful place and honor Him, then He will be found. And He will bring peace with Him as a gift—peace on earth and in every human heart.

PRAYER

Lord, thank You for the insight that personal peace and universal peace start with bringing honor to God. Forgive me that I often seek the product of peace instead of its Giver. Amen.

Sovereign Lord,
as you have promised,
you now dismiss
your servant [Simeon] in peace.
For my eyes have seen your salvation,
which you have prepared
in the sight of all people.

LUKE 2:29-31

The Bible describes Simeon as devout and righteous: devout in his relationship with God, and righteous in his relationships with God and those around him. It was revealed to Simeon that he would see the promised Messiah before he died. The Holy Spirit, who revealed the promise, guided Simeon to the Temple at the moment that Joseph and Mary arrived with the Child, Jesus. Simeon knew that He was the prophesied Messiah for whom the world had been waiting. He took the Child in his arms, praised God, and called Jesus the salvation of all people.

With the fulfillment of the promise, Simeon's life reached its destination. His task was finished. He was ready to die in peace. His words, cited above, remind us of those of the Lord Jesus. At the end of His life He said to God, "I have brought you glory on earth by completing the work you gave me to do" (John 17:4).

A person who knows that he has fulfilled his purpose no doubt experiences great peace. Few of us will receive such a distinct promise and experience its fulfillment as Simeon did. To most of us, God will reveal His plans as we go, often through the Bible, in which He speaks to us in a special and personal way.

Beyond the fulfillment of a promise, Simeon's peace was the result of having looked at the newborn Savior! We also can die in peace when we have seen Him, not with our physical eyes, but with the eyes of faith. If we have given our heart to Him, we need not fear death. We can say farewell to life in peace.

PRAYER

Lord, I want to complete to the fullest the task for which You created me. Above all, I desire to bring honor to Your Name, so that I may depart in peace. Amen.

35 THE PEACE OF FORGIVENESS

The disciples went and woke him, saying,
"Master, Master, we're going to drown!"
He got up and rebuked the wind and the
raging waters; the storm subsided,
and all was calm.

LUKE 8:24

A moment before, the lake had been still, without a ripple. Then the water began to churn like a raging fury. A sudden, rising gust of wind changed the situation completely. Peace and calm vanished instantly, replaced by turmoil.

The small fishing boat quickly filled with water. The twelve disciples—even the four experienced fishermen among them—were stricken with panic. "Master, Master, we're going to drown!" they screamed.

Jesus had remained quietly asleep in the stern. The raging elements had not alarmed the Lord of creation a bit. Waking up, He rebuked the wind and the churning water. Suddenly the storm subsided. Instantly there was a dead calm. Jesus' only reaction was, "Why are you so afraid? Where is your faith?"

The disciples were perplexed and amazed. "What kind of Man is this?" they asked, bewildered. "Even the winds and the water obey Him."

This experience had a sobering effect. The disciples in their fear had totally forgotten that the Lord over life and death Himself was aboard! To Him they had cried in despair: "Don't You care that we perish?"

Further reactions of the disciples are not recorded. Certainly they must have felt ashamed. Their thoughts may have turned back to the miracles they had recently witnessed: the young man who was raised from death to life, the many lame and crippled people who walked again before their eyes, lepers who were healed.

In nature the calm had returned, but in the hearts of the disciples, no doubt, there was still some disturbance. The greatness of the Lord graphically disclosed their smallness. This disconcerting experience did not befall unbelieving heathens, but men who loved the Lord, who left all behind to follow Him, who were in His company daily, who knew Him better than anyone else.

The Lord of nature is also the Lord of the human

heart. He can restore peace in the one as well as in the other. The peace He gives is the remedy for being disappointed with ourselves.

The disciples experienced this. Soon after the storm on the lake, Jesus and His disciples were occupied with their blessed ministry. A demon-possessed man was healed. Jesus sent out the Twelve, giving them power to heal the sick and cast out evil spirits.

Disappointment over our unbelief should not keep us from continuing in God's service. Ripened by experience and strengthened by faith, we must put our hands to the plow, more aware than ever before of God's power, for the work of the Master requires haste!

PRAYER

Lord, You know how easily our faith fails, how disappointed and inhibited we can be when we are shocked by our own unbelief. Thank You that in spite of this You want to go ahead with us, entrusting us with new tasks. Amen.

36 INNER PEACE

The Counselor, the Holy Spirit,
whom the Father will send in my name,
. . . will remind you of everything
I have said to you.
Peace I leave with you;
my peace I give you.
I do not give to you
as the world gives.
Do not let your hearts be troubled
and do not be afraid.

JOHN 14:26-27

There is a vast difference between the peace that Jesus gives and that which the world offers. The disciples saw this daily. For three years they lived with Him and experienced every situation together.

They saw that He was worshiped and reviled, that people accepted and rejected Him. He was at rest in the midst of common human circumstances such as hunger, thirst, and lack of sleep—things that can irritate people tremendously.

Even His intense expectation of death did not really disturb His peace. As He talked about leaving this world, it is no wonder that the disciples asked themselves, Where do we go from here?

Jesus told them not to be concerned or afraid: "Peace I leave with you; my peace I give you."

This peace was sufficient for their diverse characters. The quickly stirred Peter depended on it, just like the loving John. The physician, Luke, was not able to do his work acceptably without it. Neither could simple fishermen such as James and Andrew.

The peace the Lord promised was not bound to character, education, or other circumstances. This inner peace, that lived in their hearts through the Holy Spirit, expelled their fears, strengthened their characters, and increased their capabilities. It changed them.

Though Jesus Christ would no longer be on earth, His Spirit would lead and help them. He would bring the Master and His words to mind again and again.

The Spirit would point to the necessity of a walk with their Father in Heaven by word and prayer, according to Jesus' example. The source of Jesus' peace and rest would be at their disposal.

In spite of this, the disciples did not experience a glorious, uninterrupted sense of peace. One of them denied his Lord. Another betrayed Him. When Jesus was arrested, all deserted Him in fear. Circumstances temporarily removed Jesus' peace from their hearts, but confession paved the way for rest to return.

The disciples experienced, as we do, that peace is a matter of growth. We see that growth in the Book of Acts, where the disciples appeared as undaunted men who stood firm for their Lord's cause, who were not intimidated by opposition, who knew what their calling was and were faithful to that.

We will experience peace in proportion to the room we give the Holy Spirit.

 *PRAYER*

Dear Lord, may we experience the same development in our hearts as Your first disciples did. May we also grow emotionally and spiritually in Your peace. Amen.

37 PEACE IN SPITE OF DISTRESS

I have told you these things,
so that in me you may have peace.
In this world you will have trouble.
But take heart!
I have overcome the world.

JOHN 16:33

Jesus did not leave His disciples with unrealistic expectations. "There is trouble coming for you," He said. "I warn you before it comes so that you will remember what I have said."

Jesus' words were soon fulfilled. As the gospel spread quickly, people were converted and believed in Jesus Christ. This did not please Jesus' adversaries. They wanted to do away with the proclaimers of the gospel. James, the brother of Peter, was the first one to be killed by King Herod.

Peter was supposed to become the next victim. The night before his planned execution, he lay in a cell, chained between two soldiers and guarded by four squads of four soldiers each (see Acts 12). The power of the Holy Spirit, earlier poured down from heaven, had changed Peter completely. The man who, because of fear for his life, had earlier denied his Lord three times, no longer was afraid. He was not concerned about what was awaiting him tomorrow. He was asleep! What better proof of inner peace is there?

History records how some other famous people reacted in the face of death. Napoleon's personal physician wrote, "The emperor died lonely and alone. He was in terrible agony." Lenin also died in great spiritual darkness. He prayed to tables and chairs to forgive his sins. The last words of Goethe were, "More light." Buddha said, "I did not make it."[1]

Light shines brighter when the surrounding darkness is deeper. So inner peace manifests itself more clearly when outside circumstances are dark. This was the case with Peter.

Paul and Silas had a similar experience. They sat in prison with their bodies bleeding (see Acts 16). In spite of this, their inner peace was such that they sang hymns of praise to God.

The source of peace has not dwindled or dried up

after two thousand years; it is still available. Christians living under totalitarian systems prove this. Believers in China, Russia, and many other countries experience this peace daily. The spread of the gospel is often furthered by trouble instead of hindered by it.

Peace is also available to relieve the distress and misfortune none of us can escape, such as illness, adversity, unemployment, and misunderstanding. Each one of us can experience peace in the midst of trouble over and over again.

Problems are bound to come. But God will be adequate for any and every situation. Jesus' victory over the spirit of this world will strip fear of its sting. Christ will give peace.

PRAYER

Lord, today I pray for those people who live under totalitarian regimes, that unbelievers may be reached with the gospel, and that Christians may increase in faith, wisdom, and steadfastness, remaining faithful and winning others with their testimony. Amen.

FOOTNOTE
1. Taken from a tract, "The Last Words of Famous Men" (Emmeloord, The Netherlands: Operation Mobilisation).

38 MESSENGERS OF PEACE

Jesus came and stood among them and said, "Peace be with you!" . . . The disciples were overjoyed when they saw the Lord. Again Jesus said, "Peace be with you! As the Father has sent me, I am sending you."

JOHN 20:19-21

"In me you may have peace" (John 16:33). Those were Jesus' parting words to His disciples before His death. "Peace be with you" was His greeting when they met for the first time after His resurrection.

Between the two events, that statement was severely tested: considering Jesus, who they thought to be destined for the throne, but who instead was laid in a grave; considering the disappointment of the disciples with themselves when they left Him alone in His time of gravest need; considering the strange empty sepulchre and the unbelievable news about His resurrection; considering the proclamation of the gospel, which seemed to be senseless now that everything had turned out to be an apparent debacle; considering the oppression of the Jewish leaders, because of which they met behind closed doors. The future had never looked darker.

Then the disciples discovered that Jesus was not dead. He was alive! To their happy surprise, things were more hopeful than they had looked before. What had seemed to be a closed door appeared to be a wide open door. Peace, so far tasted only in the circle of Jesus' closest acquaintances, began to spread over the entire world. People of all places were confronted with it.

And they, the disciples, were privileged to be the first proclaimers of this good news! With the same authority with which God sent his Son into this world, Christ sent His disciples: "As the Father has sent me, I am sending you" (John 20:21).

They did not derive their competence from themselves, but from Him. In His power they preached the gospel, remitted sins, healed the sick, and raised the dead. And they understood what had sounded mysterious before: "I tell you the truth, anyone who has faith in me will do what I have been doing. He will do even greater things than these, because I am going to the Father" (John 14:12).

The disciples also received the gift of the Holy Spirit. He lives in the heart of every believer today and so multiplies the number of messengers of peace, creating a chain of people that encompasses the world.

There is a legend about how joyful it was in Heaven when Jesus returned there. The angels shouted for joy because He had accomplished His task on earth. Then a little angel stepped forward and asked, "Lord, how will the gospel be preached down there from now on? Who will tell the people what You have done for them now that You have returned to Heaven?"

"I left My disciples behind to do this," Jesus answered.

"And if they fail, is there an alternative?"

"No, if they fail, there is no alternative. Then the people will not hear the good news."

The first disciples didn't fail. Within a number of years the gospel was heard in the farthest corners of the world. The spread of the gospel still depends on common men and women, on young people, even children, who in their own circles pass on the message of God's peace.

Is the good news still being passed on where you live and work?

=========================== *PRAYER* ===========================

Lord, it is an awesome realization that the proclamation of the gospel rests in the hands of people like me. May the good news of salvation through Jesus Christ be clearly seen and heard in me where I live and work. Amen.

39 PEACE WITH GOD

He was delivered over to death for our sins and was raised to life for our justification. Therefore, since we have been justified through faith, we have peace with God through our Lord Jesus Christ.

ROMANS 4:25-5:1

The peace that Paul announced in Romans did not follow an agreement between two equal parties. It was not a treaty based on certain conditions that must be met by both sides. Here two extremes became reconciled that principally could never be brought into harmony: the holy God and the sinful individual.

Many people neglect this peace. They think that they can live without it, or can find it elsewhere, perhaps through good relationships, education, or a successful career. In time they find that their hearts are not satisfied by any of these, for God has created the human heart so that it can find rest only in Him.

Others seek this peace diligently. They torture themselves, pray till their knees bleed, or give up everything for it. Or they search after inner peace through deceptive solutions such as alcohol, drugs, religious cults, and sexual experiences. These gods prove to be deaf and mute. They don't have the expected answers.

Still others feel unworthy, sinful, guilty. For that reason they probably give up all hope of peace. Paul was among these. He called himself "the worst of sinners" because he persecuted the Christians (1 Timothy 1:16). For that reason, it is encouraging that he wrote about peace with God and being justified by faith. He stated that every individual by nature is a sinner who falls short of the glory of God (see Romans 3:23). Such a person cannot partake of God's peace.

Paul wrote further that sinners are brought into a right relationship with God through faith in Jesus Christ. Peace between God and man is being offered on the basis of God's forgiving love. People who accept that gift are declared righteous before God (see Romans 4:24).

Righteousness is more than forgiveness and remittance of punishment. It means that any sin ever committed by the believer is totally covered and buried (see Romans 4:7). Because of Jesus Christ, the sinner stands before God as though no sin ever took place.

Small wonder that such people are called blessed. They live in peace with God. Greater happiness is not possible. Neither is there anything more conducive to human welfare and well-being. Peace with God penetrates every sphere of life. It illuminates all our relationships.

Peace with God is the point where true life starts and for which life is destined. Blessed is the individual who knows this from experience!

 PRAYER

Lord, I realize that my only hope for peace with God is by believing that Jesus Christ died for me. I acknowledge that I am a sinner and I accept His sacrifice for me. Thank You that now I am declared righteous in Your sight. Amen.

40 WHERE PEACE BEGINS

Do not repay anyone evil for evil. Be careful to do what is right in the eyes of everybody. If it is possible, as far as it depends on you, live at peace with everyone.

ROMANS 12:17-18

The Bible is realistic, as is the Apostle Paul in Romans. He did not say all our relationships would be equal. There are those we love spontaneously and others with whom we may have some trouble.

Jesus Himself proved that there are different levels of human relationships. We have closer relationships with some people than with others. Jesus chose His twelve disciples from among many, and among the Twelve He had His bosom friend, John.

In spite of all good intentions, peace between two people can be difficult to achieve, as it was for the writer of Psalm 120:7—"I am a man of peace; but when I speak, they are for war."

We must strive after peace and harmony with others. If we do all that is possible, but are rejected, then the other party is responsible. We are not to blame and should carry no guilt in the matter.

It is evident that peace in its various applications, such as in the family, church, and society, begins in essence between two individuals. Therefore we personally must do all we can to enhance peace. The world is waiting for it.

What can help us achieve this? The Bible shows the way. Without this guide, our personal mission of peace does not have much hope.

We should begin by praying for peace-loving wisdom from above (see James 3:17). In answer to prayer, God will give insight, love, and the sorely needed tact. We will find the willingness to make the sacrifices peace demands from us. That is the first step.

The second step is to apply the Scripture that teaches us to overcome selfishness and to look after the welfare of others, to overcome rivalry and arrogance, to be modest and think higher of others than of ourselves (see Philippians 2:3), and, as Jesus said, to do to others as we would have them do to us (see Matthew 7:12). Then peace will draw near with quick steps.

This doesn't mean that we should cover up differences. On the contrary. It is wise and a proof of sober thinking to be realistic. It is sensible to admit that irritations and frustrations are continually around the corner.

We must understand that people differ from us, that they may think differently about all kinds of things. Even Christians don't think alike on many points of biblical exegesis. Accepting this provides a basis for peace with others.

Regarding background, education, personality and spiritual maturity, one can hardly think of a more varied group than Jesus' twelve disciples. There was Matthew, the former tax gatherer who had been despised for colaboring with the Romans, and the fiery nationalist, Simon the zealot. Impetuous Peter had to work next to the slow-believing Thomas. Despite these differences, they had to carry out a united task, often under much opposition.

The Lord said specifically to them, "Love one another. As I have loved you, so you must love one another."

Absence of love is the main problem. Peace begins when loving one another begins. When mutual love breaks through, then harmony and happiness increase. Through us the world sees God. And that is exactly the purpose for which we were created.

PRAYER

Lord, I must admit honestly that I often struggle with this kind of peace. Teach me real love and true understanding for others, especially for those who are near to me. Amen.

41 PEACEFUL CONDUCT

*For the kingdom of God is not
a matter of eating and drinking,
but of righteousness, peace and joy in
the Holy Spirit, because anyone
who serves Christ in this way is pleasing
to God and approved by men.*

ROMANS 14:17-18

Christians who take their faith seriously still find it hard sometimes to maintain peace with one another. This is because they hold different standards of conduct based on what they believe. They judge one another according to what behavior they think is or is not permitted. This happens between Christians who attend the same church, as well as between Christians who live in different countries.

Years ago Scandinavian Christians were shocked when they saw English believers playing soccer. Belgian and Dutch women found it difficult to overlook the heavy facial makeup of their American sisters. At the same time, Americans asked themselves if a German behind a tall glass of beer could indeed be a Christian.

Within each country there are conflicting views. In the Netherlands, for instance, Christians used to differ in opinions concerning bicycling on Sunday. Smoking cigarettes and drinking alcohol are acceptable to some, but still taboo for others.

To the Christians in Rome, animals sacrificed to idols were a problem. There was a difference of opinion whether one was allowed to eat them or not. One group thought the meat to be contaminated and thus forbidden. Others said there were no so-called gods, only one God. Consequently, this food did not differ from any other, and there was nothing wrong in eating it.

The Apostle Paul did not handle the situation by simply pronouncing a statement about this difference of opinion. He pointed to something more important, the truth that people who think differently should get along with one another. The behavior in question was of secondary importance. Paul made it clear that being a Christian in the deepest sense doesn't depend on what we eat or drink. Faith is based on having a right relationship with God through Jesus Christ.

Someone who, by grace, experiences a right relationship with God will also aim for a right relationship with his fellow Christians. He will allow others the right to their own convictions.

Are you willing to abstain from something that offends somebody else? In other words, can you leave something undone or give it up in order not to hinder another Christian who may be younger or weaker, even when this activity is not wrong in your own eyes?

For instance, will you abstain from smoking or drinking wine among those for whom these things are wrong? Are you willing to go without lipstick where use of it is detested? Can you put your own desires aside for the name of Christ? Will you be the least, because He became the least of all?

In Romans 14 there are some other indications of how you can get along when you differ in opinion, and so maintain peace with one another. Verse 18 points to the willingness to be a servant of God. In other words, are you looking for the honor of God or for your own right? He or she who puts the honor of God first will be tolerant of a fellow Christian and so receive his respect, even if the difference of opinion remains.

Verse 19 indicates that peace grows out of mutual edification. Are you willing to ask yourself how you can serve the other person in such a situation?

When you do these things to serve others rather than advance your cause—and that is a matter of practice and growth—you not only experience peace, but joy as well, since for the love of Christ you were able to act for the well-being of others. My experience proves that such joy is much richer than the "loss" of what I give up.

=========== *PRAYER* ===========

Lord, give me love for things pertaining to You, and sensitivity to the beliefs of others. Grant me a willingness to set my own desires aside. Amen.

42 DEVOTION TO PEACE

Let us therefore make every effort
to do what leads to peace
and to mutual edification. . . .
It is better not to . . . do anything . . .
that will cause your brother to fall.

ROMANS 14:19, 21

Peace has seldom been so fragile as right now. A worldwide conflagration seems close at hand.

Heads of state in the East and the West question one another's intentions. Leaders of peace groups make one another look suspect.

In the Sermon on the Mount, Jesus called the peacemakers blessed, after He said, "Blessed are the pure in heart" (Matthew 5:8-9). Outer peace follows an inner, peaceful state of mind. Peace on a large scale originates from harmony between people.

The price for peace requires no less than an unflagging devotion of every individual personally. But the goal is well worth it! To two groups of spiritual leaders who found it hard to live together peacefully, Jesus gave this solution: "Love your neighbor as yourself" (Matthew 22:39).

Peace begins close at home, by devoting ourselves to the welfare of someone else, by listening carefully, and trying to imagine the other person's position, by being sensitive and considerate of his or her needs, by accepting and respecting the individual's personality.

Working for peace requires humility and a willingness to be corrected ourselves. It requires courage to serve others with positive criticism, if needed. Rich possibilities for mutual building up exist in such a relationship.

In doing so, we should keep in mind that a human heart is locked (often permanently) when confronted in a self-centered way. It leaves no room for the other person, who feels shut out. Feelings of irritation become a small step to personal or general discord. Ill feelings multiply easily and consequently, peace—whether in our family, the church, or society, or even in the entire world—is destroyed.

One of the wonderful things about the Bible is that it offers examples of its truths. The story of David and Jonathan exemplifies one such truth. They were two people between whom peace seemed nearly impossible.

David's life was repeatedly threatened by Jonathan's father, King Saul. In spite of this, David didn't grow bitter. Jonathan remained his friend. David, on the other side, ascended to the throne that Jonathan should have inherited. Despite this, Jonathan wasn't jealous. He had the best for David in mind.

Every ingredient to drive two people apart was there. Yet after many centuries, their friendship is proverbial instead. They parted one from the other in peace (see 1 Samuel 20:42) because they had covenanted their friendship in a bond with God.

Peace begins when we purposefully build relationships. And these are most likely to succeed if our starting point is God.

PRAYER

Lord, give me a mind that is attentive to others. Help me to think of the best for them first instead of the best for myself. Search my heart and mind and show me how to improve my efforts to build others up. Amen.

43 OVERFLOWING WITH HOPE

May the God of hope
fill you with all joy and peace
as you trust in him,
so that you may overflow with hope
by the power of the Holy Spirit.

ROMANS 15:13

When we look at the world around us, we find that overflowing hope is in complete disagreement with present reality. Life today is not characterized by hope and joy, but by fear and questions regarding survival. John F. Kennedy once said, "It remains to be seen whether civilization will be mended before it is ended."[1]

This question is of deep concern to many. Is the hour glass of time running out? Are we facing the end of the world? Are we hearing in the distance the hoofbeats of the horses that will predict God's judgment (see Revelation 6)?

Newspaper headlines, radio, and television bring daily news of little hope. To the contrary, they offer reports of war, starvation, revolts, oppression, and murder.

The earth itself gives no reason for optimism. It is affected by a growing number of earthquakes and famines in many places. It suffers from the effects of polluted water, air, and soil and other environmental destruction.

We are regularly confronted by new inventions and striking technological possibilities. Yet at the same time, instead of life on a higher plane, resistance against spiritual and moral decay is visibly falling off. Estrangement between parents and children increases. The divorce rate is growing alarmingly worse. Unfaithfulness in marriage and sexual permissiveness are increasingly acceptable. Hopelessness and apathy grow stronger. We are presented with a picture of despair.

What, then, is the hope about which Paul spoke in Romans 15, the hope that is fed by joy and peace? The previous verse (15:12) referred to the rule of Jesus Christ, the Messiah, and His coming reign of peace when the world will be governed by righteousness and faithfulness, when evil, sickness, death, anger, and racial discrimination will not exist anymore, when war will cease and swords will be beaten into plowshares.

Faith is the door through which peace, joy, and hope enter a life. A person who believes in Christ experiences peace with God. He has hope for the future because the same Lord Jesus Christ who came to earth to reconcile men with God has promised that He will return. Then He will make everything new. New! Our text leaves no doubt for those who trust in Christ.

People who choose not to believe in Him will have to give account for their choice and bear the consequences thereof. That will mean condemnation to hell. About this there is not the slightest doubt. Therefore, it is wise while it is still possible, to choose Jesus Christ—NOW. He stands at the door of our heart and desires to be invited in. Those who do this receive joy and peace and the certainty of a glorious future.

PRAYER

Lord, thank You for the wonderful promise of Christ's return and for a future when evil, pain, and death will be no more. May my heart increasingly overflow with hope in view of this glorious prospect. Amen.

FOOTNOTE
1. Quoted by Billy Graham, *Decision*, January 1984, page 2.

44 REFRESHING FELLOWSHIP

For when we came into Macedonia,
this body of ours had no rest,
but we were harassed at every turn—
conflicts on the outside, fears within.
But God, who comforts the downcast,
comforted us by the coming of Titus.

2 CORINTHIANS 7:5-6

The life of the Apostle Paul consisted of much traveling and a very irregular schedule. His body consequently received little rest. The emotional and spiritual tensions he had to deal with were worse than this lack of physical rest. Paul often encountered misunderstanding and suspicion. Some people even doubted his apostolic mission. It is easy to understand why Paul felt in danger of becoming disheartened. (Other Bible versions use synonyms like *weak, small,* and *humble* for downcast. It is remarkable that to receive help through rest, one first has to be humble.)

God the Father, however, knew what His child needed. He comforted Paul through the person of Titus, who had been converted through Paul's preaching and later became his co-laborer.

Through a meeting with fellow Christians, Titus had recently received new courage and joy himself. Therefore he was in a cheerful mood when he visited Paul. Titus's friendship brought Paul rest. Their time together turned out to be spiritually and physically refreshing to Paul, and a stimulus to tackle his work again with renewed vigor.

The sense of rest that one person can convey to another can hardly be overestimated. People need one another, not only in important things such as functioning in society, church, and the home, but also in small things such as when feeling discouraged or depressed. We cannot do without one another. We are privileged when we have friends who meet such needs, especially when they are like-minded in the faith.

=== *PRAYER* ===

Lord, thank You for like-minded friends who attend to my needs. Thank You for the encouragement and stimulus they present. Help me detect this need in others and be humble enough to seek help myself. Amen.

45 A MATTER OF CHOICE

*But the fruit of the Spirit
is love, joy, peace,
patience, kindness, goodness,
faithfulness, gentleness and self-control.
Against such things there is no law.
Those who belong to Christ Jesus
have crucified the sinful nature.*

GALATIANS 5:22-24

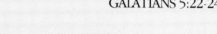

The Bible compares our life with a tree. Just like a tree, our life can and should be green and bear fruit. The life-tree of a Christian should produce a richly varied harvest.

In the list of the fruit of the Spirit, peace is preceded by love and joy, both of which point to inner experiences. Peace is followed by expressions of character such as patience, kindness, goodness, faithfulness, gentleness, and self-control.

Peace and feelings of well-being grow from love, which in turn prevents jealousy and bragging. Love for our fellow man means that we do not quickly lose patience or exhibit a bad temper. Love doesn't want to hurt. It nurses no grudges. Love enables us to love the other person as ourselves. And love does much more, as we can read in 1 Corinthians 13.

When we recognize the fruit of the Spirit within ourselves, we consequently are grateful and happy. We experience inner peace and rest. But how do we produce such fruit? How can our character change in such a way that it produces virtues we often are missing?

In Galatians 5:16-21, we read first of all that this is a matter of choice. We can choose to yield to the Holy Spirit, resulting in His fruit. Or we can yield to "the desires of the sinful nature," that is, desires of our senses, which are infected by the evil one. In that case the fruit is not love, joy, and peace. On the contrary, we exhibit immorality, impurity, indecency, anger, ill temper, jealousy, and selfish ambition, to name some sinful acts.

Galatians 6:7-8 makes a comparison with the sowing of grain: what we sow, we will reap. Those who sow to please their sinful natures, who give in to selfish desires, will reap death and destruction. But if we sow to please the Holy Spirit, then as a result He will produce His fruit in us.

Peace is not a vague emotion, to be compared with

a refreshing spring rain that unexpectedly showers down on us. Peace is the result of an act of the will, of daily conscious action, of considering others, and choosing God.

This peace is not acquired all at once. It comes step by step. It is a result of development and growth. To experience the peace promised here, all of us need the help of the Holy Spirit. He alone can help us to know this peace to the full and in all its rich variety. Some people are by nature more peace-conscious than others. One individual is more inhibited by selfishness and other vices than his neighbor. But no one is so peace-loving of himself that he can manage without God's Spirit. However, no one falls so far short in this that there is no hope.

PRAYER

Lord, cause me to be a tree on which peace and other good fruit grow. May my character develop after Your image, by the power of the Holy Spirit within me. Amen.

Do not be anxious about anything, but in everything, by prayer and petition, with thanksgiving, present your requests to God. And the peace of God, which transcends all understanding, will guard your hearts and your minds in Christ Jesus.

PHILIPPIANS 4:6-7

People worry, sometimes about futilities, like the woman standing before the mirror, who discovered two new tiny wrinkles in her face—and wept! Others have anxious fears about things such as water, spiders, or heights. Many fearfully step aboard an airplane or dread old age. There are people who cannot enjoy themselves, fearful of trouble that may never occur. They lessen their enjoyment of life by carrying burdens God never put on their shoulders.

On the other hand, we face problems our forebears didn't know about. There are increasing threats of terror and war in the world. There is a clouded future in view of the downward economic trend and unemployment in many places. The environment is in a precarious condition due to the unrealistic demands we have made upon it. Young couples don't want children because they doubt the future existence of humanity. Many ask, "Will we live to see the year 2000?" There is a flight from reality to alcohol, crime, and drugs. Suicide, especially among youth, takes alarming numbers. Present thinking about abortion and euthanasia reveals how relative the worth of human life has become in the minds of many.

The Bible teaches that we are not to worry about all these anxieties and fears. Worry and concern don't help, and we shouldn't burden today with tomorrow's cares. Living one day at a time is a heavy enough weight for a person to carry. Most important of all, God knows what we need. He cares royally for the birds and the flowers. Will He then forget His children (see Matthew 6:25-34)?

It is not relevant whether our worries are valid or unnecessary. What matters is that we shift the center of gravity, that we transfer it to God. Think of standing on a scale while carrying a rock weighing forty pounds. The scale carries the total weight whether or not you hold the stone. For you, however, it makes all the difference whether you hold the rock or put it down.

In order to get rid of our worries, we must talk them over with God and leave them with Him. We should not pick them up again after our "Amen." To lay them down and leave them is difficult. It requires practice and growth. In fact, it takes an entire lifetime to learn this.

Thanking God for answered prayer, even small things, plays a part in overcoming anxiety. Gratitude makes us observant of what God does. It is important, not only to God, but also to us. It strengthens our trust, and gives us joy. Gratitude is excellent medicine to prevent worry. The inner peace that comes with thankfulness drives worry away. The opposite is also true. Thankful people are less vulnerable to worry. So the way is prepared for inner peace, not because life is without cares, but because we know God. Prayer doesn't always change the situation, but does change our thoughts about it.

The eldest son of Momma Kwong, a Chinese Christian, was tortured to death. When her husband was taken to prison, she and her youngest children had no one to care for them. This put her in a very difficult position. She wrote in a letter, "Jesus said, 'My yoke is easy and My burden is light.' I have discovered that the cross of our Lord is heavy as long as you look at it. But as soon as you start to carry it, it becomes light."

As a consequence of her suffering and the way she responded to it, Momma Kwong now travels around the world to tell people that God gives peace in troublesome situations. Such ministries are available to those who exchange their worries for God's peace!

===================== *PRAYER* =====================

Lord, You know how hard it is not to worry at times. You know exactly the problems that are bothering me right now. Teach me to surrender, to be grateful, to enjoy Your peace, and to pass it on to others. Amen.

47 PRACTICING PEACE

May the Lord direct your hearts into God's love and Christ's perseverance. . . . Now may the Lord of peace himself give you peace at all times and in every way.

2 THESSALONIANS 3:5,16

Each of Paul's thirteen letters begins with a greeting of peace. Some, like this one to the Christians in the Greek city of Thessalonica, end the same way. These words were full of meaning. Paul was reminding the Thessalonians that the Lord, the author of peace, would give His peace always, in every way and under all circumstances. The Thessalonians needed this encouragement badly. They were people who suffered from oppression and persecution, who were confronted with the problem of immorality, who were full of sorrow because of loved ones who had died, who lived among difficult and pagan people, and who were confronted by false religious teachers and people with warped minds.

Paul's words referred back to the reality of the night in which Christ was born. The Lord who gives peace, because He Himself is peace, was born to command peace. It is the same peace of which the Lord later would say to His disciples, "Peace I leave with you; my peace I give you" (John 14:27). "I have told you these things, so that in me you may have peace. In this world you will have trouble. But take heart! I have overcome the world" (John 16:33).

The Thessalonians claimed this peace, and proved it to be applicable and sufficient in their varied situations. This peace lifted them above their problems. In spite of pressure and adversity, their faith grew so that they became examples to others.

Even today we can draw comfort from the experiences of those who have gone before us. We can try to follow their good example, learn not to lose heart, and nurture hope.

Circumstances in the eighties are far from rosy. The world finds itself in chaos. Many a family is in a crisis. The church is often at a loss for the right answers. Small wonder that our hearts lack peace and are full of uncertainty. But in spite of this we can experience the Lord's peace continually, and in every way.

Peace must be practical and practiced! We best begin each new day with God, reading His Word and praying. Then we can think back to this quiet time throughout the day to claim His peace when unrest and discord are knocking at our door. We must remind ourselves that no situation we find ourselves in is beyond the range of God's interest in us.

 *PRAYER*

Lord, thank You that Your promise of peace for all times and in every way is still valid. May this peace penetrate our hearts and minds, in spite of pressure and adversity. Teach us gratitude. Amen.

48 PEACE THROUGH PRAYER

I urge, then, first of all, that requests, prayers, intercession and thanksgiving be made for everyone—for kings and all those in authority, that we may live peaceful and quiet lives in all godliness and holiness.

1 TIMOTHY 2:1-2

Ve human beings are willing to work hard to achieve an undisturbed life. One man looked for years for a quiet spot to live. Finally he felt that he had found what he was looking for. He sold everything he had and left for the Falkland Islands, shortly before the war between Argentina and Great Britain broke out there! Instead of having peace and rest, he found himself in one of the most uneasy spots on the globe.

The elements for restful and peaceful living are available in our time. People—in the West, at least—are better educated and live longer than ever before, which should enhance mutual respect and lessen prejudice. Modern technology supplies us with the means to improve communication. Financially we are better off in some ways than before. Traveling abroad increases international understanding.

In spite of this, discord, unhappiness, and misunderstanding are on the increase. Undoubtedly there are various causes responsible for this. Possibly the main one is that we have forgotten or neglected what is most important: prayer. We have not sufficiently availed ourselves of prayer.

Paul makes a striking appeal for intercession "on behalf of all men" (NASB), especially for those in positions of authority and leadership of nations. Undisturbed peace and stability are dependent upon God.

Intensive prayer, consisting of petitions, intercession, and thanksgiving, is born and developed in our daily walk with God. It grows in strength in the measure that we develop the habit.

Such prayer includes specific names and facts. It is personal and practical. The petitions are based on promises of God's Word, so that He will answer. Thanksgiving is an integral part of it all.

Why is prayer for a Christian so exceedingly important? Because God makes Himself dependent upon it! Two passages of Scripture prove this: "He saw that there was no one . . . to intercede" (Isaiah 59:16); "I looked for a man among them who would build up the wall and stand before me in the gap on behalf of the land so I would not have to destroy it" (Ezekiel 22:30).

It is not exaggerating to say that prayer moves the Hand that governs the world. One of the most remarkable examples is that of Moses. When the Israelites bowed down before an idol in the shape of a golden calf, this so kindled God's wrath that He wanted to destroy the entire nation. His patience had run out!

Moses interceded for the continued existence of the people. He humbly based his request on God's faithfulness, fearing that otherwise the adversaries of God would bring dishonor to His name. A miracle resulted. "Then the Lord relented and did not bring on his people the disaster he had threatened" (Exodus 32:14). Judgment was withheld. God changed His plans—because of one human being who prayed. God's blessings to the Israelites are recorded in Psalm 106:23, where we read, "So he said he would destroy them—had not Moses, his chosen one, stood in the breach before him."

Moses proved that one person standing in the breach in prayer can make the difference between life and death of an entire nation. Here we find not a nation praying for its leaders, but a leader interceding for his people. Both are needed.

PRAYER

Lord, forgive me that I haven't influenced my country, church, and society with prayer as I should. Help me to improve my prayer life, so that increased godliness may be experienced in the world around me. Amen.

49 CHOICES FOR PEACE

Flee the evil desires of youth,
and pursue righteousness,
faith, love and peace,
along with those who call on the Lord
out of a pure heart. . . .
The Lord's servant . . .
must be kind to everyone,
able to teach, not resentful.

2 TIMOTHY 2:22-24

The Apostle Paul wrote two letters to Timothy, his "son in the faith." In the second letter, Paul explained that peace and harmony between people rests on three pillars. Each one of them is a personal choice.

First, Timothy should choose to stay away from the evil desires of youth, that is, endless disputes about controversial issues, because fighting for his own rights and views would be harmful to unity and peace.

Timothy was responsible for the church in Ephesus, a heavy task. There were false teachers in the church who made an impression by their complicated and seemingly profound views. These circumstances increased Timothy's responsibilities and made his work heavier. He easily could have wasted time in endless and purposeless talks and thus increased the unrest in the church. Paul warned Timothy to choose not to do this. Paul knew that endless debates about differences of opinion lead to hot heads and cold hearts. The results are jealousy, slander, and insinuation, and sometimes schisms and separation.

Paul urged that Timothy deliberately choose to pursue peace, in the company of righteousness, faith, and love. He should untiringly be dedicated to peace, an active involvement requiring great effort. Paul advised Timothy to choose to give himself to people who also loved the Lord. Colaboring with other dedicated Christians would make him stronger.

In the two letters addressed to Timothy, Paul repeatedly exhorted him to choose to spend time in regular intake and application of the Scriptures. The apostle understood that peace with those around Timothy and peace in the local church was dependent on the peace God gives to those who obey his Word.

The writer of Psalm 119 spoke from experience in answer to the question, "How can a young man keep his way pure?" In other words, how does he keep from sinning? He gave the answer himself: "By living according to your word" (verse 9). "I have hidden your word in my heart that I might not sin against you" (verse 11).

Living according to God's Word keeps us from sin. Sin, on the other hand, can keep us from living according to that Word. The best defense against evil is Scripture. When our thoughts are full of the words of God, then sin has less chance. Turn against sin. Instead, choose good company and regular fellowship with the Word of God to enhance peace. This is of highest importance for Christian leaders, whether they are young or old. It is important for all people of every position and every age. Our choices determine what we desire, do, are, and become—even today.

PRAYER

Lord, I pray that Christian leaders will make right choices, apply Your Word, preach it faithfully and with conviction, and so be examples to their flocks. Amen.

50 ENTERING HIS REST

Therefore, since the promise
of entering his rest still stands,
let us be careful that none of you
be found to have fallen short of it. . . .
Now we who have believed
enter that rest. . . .
Let us, therefore,
make every effort to enter that rest.

HEBREWS 4:1,3,11

The author of Hebrews wrote about total, perfect, and lasting rest, the rest that Jesus Christ Himself spoke of at the cross when He said, "It is finished." Christians are partakers of this rest. They experience rest in their relationship with God because their sins are forgiven. They rest because they do not need to exert themselves to earn their salvation. This rest points to eternal, heavenly rest yet to come, which was instituted by God after the completion of creation.

Why must we be careful not to fall short of this rest? Because this has happened in history. The Israelites are one example. They wandered through the desert for forty years as a result of their unbelief. And this is still happening today. Rest is offered to everyone, but many do not enter into it because of disobedience or unbelief.

The rest God extends to man is not automatically given to everyone. It is bound to definite conditions that must be accepted. Those conditions can be studied by every individual, for God had them openly recorded in His Book, the Bible. To receive rest, a person must show personal faith in Jesus Christ and live one's life in obedience to Him.

We must take these conditions seriously, since we will have to give account for our deeds. Let every right-minded person, therefore, ask himself, How do I react to the rest that is offered to me?

PRAYER

Keep me from not fully entering into Your rest because of disobedience or unbelief. Help me to take inventory and to apply Your Word daily to every aspect of my life, so that I may not be ashamed when You ask me to give account. Amen.

51 HEAVENLY RESTLESSNESS

And the four beasts . . .
rest not day and night,
saying, Holy, holy, holy,
Lord God Almighty,
which was, and is,
and is to come. . . .
Thou art worthy, O Lord,
to receive glory
and honour and power:
for thou hast created all things,
and for thy pleasure
they are and were created.

REVELATION 4:8,11, KJV

Human history clearly does not end in destruction and chaos, but in the glorification of God. This heavenly vision recorded in Revelation reveals Him as the pivotal point of all of creation and world history. In the verses quoted above we find not rest, but restlessness instead—holy, heavenly restlessness. The heavenly creatures cannot keep their mouths—indeed, their very beings— from exalting the glory of God.

There is restlessness in Heaven because the holiness of the triune God—Father, Son, and Holy Spirit—has to be proclaimed without interruption. He is the Almighty, Creator and Keeper of the universe and every living thing. He is the Unchangeable, the Eternal, who was and who is and who is to come: the Lord! Therefore, He is worthy to receive honor without ceasing. This eternal Lord is the Savior, who transformed sinful people into children of God.

People of every race and nationality will not stop thanking and worshiping Christ in eternity. He who humbled Himself in the deepest hell is now exalted in the highest Heaven. Therefore, all that is heard in Heaven is, "Glory be to God."

We cannot do better than, by faith, to join this future heavenly host and exclaim joyfully, GLORY, YES, GLORY BE TO GOD!

PRAYER

Lord, Thou art worthy to receive glory and honor and power; for Thou hast created all things and for Thy pleasure they are and were created. May my heart, soul, and body bring honor and pleasure to Thy holy name! Amen.

52 REST AND REWARD

Then I [John] heard a voice from heaven say, "Write: Blessed are the dead who die in the Lord from now on."

"Yes," says the Spirit, "they will rest from their labor, for their deeds will follow them."

REVELATION 14:13

The Bible leaves no doubt that there is life after death. Man is created for eternity. The earthly life is but an overture, a prelude of the reality to come. Blessed—happy, to be envied—are the dead "who die in the Lord." They are people who during their earthly life believed in Jesus Christ as their Savior and Lord. When they exchange the temporal for the eternal, their work is done forever. They finally have rest. All the troubles and tensions of their earthly existence are behind them. They have arrived at their eternal destination. They are HOME!

The Scriptures paint a frightening alternative for people who do not seek God during their lifetime: "And the smoke of their torment rises for ever and ever. There is no rest day or night" (Revelation 14:11).

What a contrast!

The dead who die in the Lord not only enjoy eternally the absence of unrest, pain, and sorrow, but they also are rewarded: "Their deeds will follow them."

Man is free to live his life according to his own choices. But he has to keep in mind that there will be a future settling of accounts. Every individual will—justly—be rewarded according to his deeds. The measuring staff will be administered according to his attitude towards the Lord Jesus Christ.

True rest awaits only those who during their life on earth took God seriously. Without Him there is no real rest, in the present or in the future.

PRAYER

Lord, thank You for eternal rest to come for those who believe in Jesus Christ. Thank You for promised heavenly reward for service done on earth. Thank You for the reality of future life with You. Certainly the best is still to come! Amen.

SCRIPTURE INDEX

Old Testament

New Testament

30. Matthew 11:28
31. Matthew 11:29-30
32. Mark 6:30-31
33. Luke 2:13-14
34. Luke 2:29-31
35. Luke 8:24
36. John 14:26-27
37. John 16:33
38. John 20:19-21
39. Romans 4:25-5:1
40. Romans 12:17-18
41. Romans 14:17-18
42. Romans 14:19,21
43. Romans 15:13
44. 2 Corinthians 7:5-6
45. Galatians 5:22-24
46. Philippians 4:6-7
47. 2 Thessalonians 3:5,16
48. 1 Timothy 2:1-2
49. 2 Timothy 2:22-24
50. Hebrews 4:1,3,11
51. Revelation 4:8,11
52. Revelation 14:13